Beautiful Mountains
For Kids

Nature Books for Kids
By K. Bennett
Mendon Cottage Books

JD-Biz Publishing

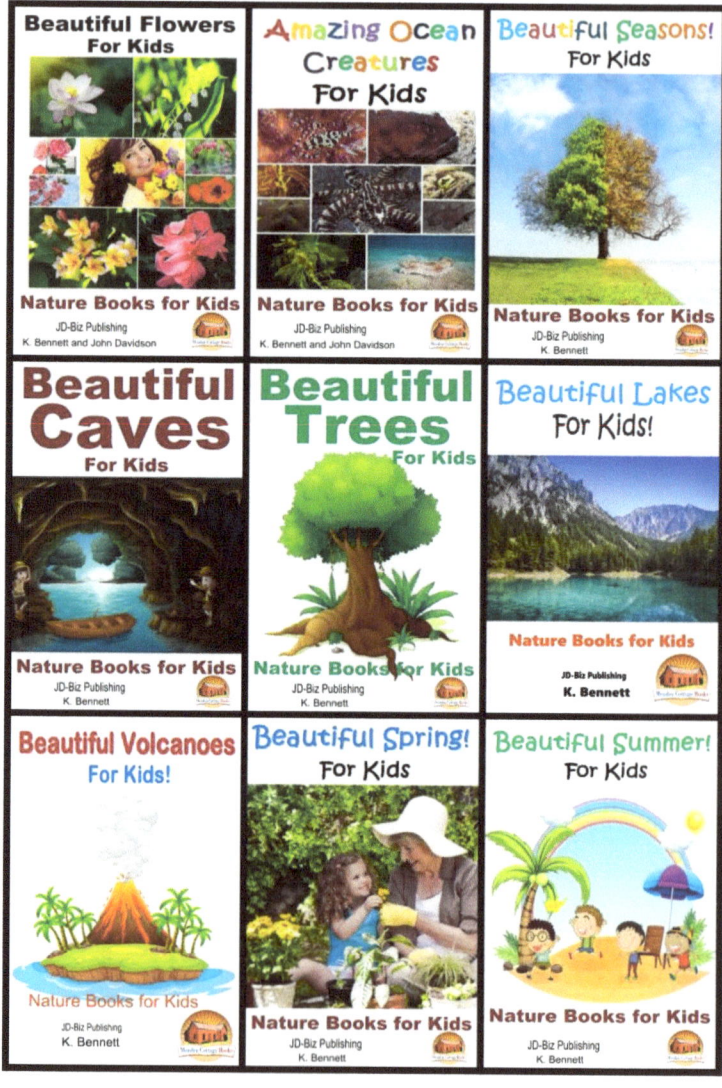

Table of Contents

Introduction

"Every mountain top is within reach if you just keep climbing." ~Barry Finlay

***

Mountains make the world more beautiful and a very interesting place to live. Some mountains are big and others are small. Did you know planet earth is full of mountains?

Many animals live on mountains and many people love to hike them just for fun or adventure. How about you? How do you feel about mountains?

If someone asked you what is a mountain… what would you say? The easy definition of a mountain is a large chunk of land pushed upwards that forms sharp peaks on top.

Let say…a mountain comes up from the ground and is higher than everything else around it. They are not hills because they are bigger than hills. And mountains don't like to be alone. They like to be with other mountains!

How can we tell a mountain and hill apart? The difference is the height of a mountain has to rise more than 1,000 feet above the things around it to be called a mountain.

Mountains are formed by the movement of Tectonic plates. In our book **Beautiful Volcanoes**, we talked about these plates.
"If you dig all the way inside the earth, you will find something that looks like a giant puzzle with lots of different parts. The parts we want to discover are called: "tectonic plates.""

There are eight important plates on the planet and there are some smaller ones too. These big plates move around all the time and soon pressure starts to build. *Geography4kids.com* says "to think of the plates like the skin of planet earth."

But how does it work?

Easy science for kids says to think of it like this: When two cars run into each other head on, what happens? Did you think of how much the car crumples up in the front? This is what scientist says happens to the mountain and that's why they looked so crumpled up!

Scientists also say some mountains are formed because of volcanic eruptions. When rocks melt inside the earth, it pushes up to the surface and turns into lava. Then the lava and the hot dust from the volcano cooled down and soon mountains start to grow. This takes a very long time. How long? Millions of years long!

What else can we learn?

Mountains are everywhere on planet earth and even in the ocean. Did you know some of the highest mountains are at the bottom of the sea? Some islands are even at the tops of mountains!

Do you think it might be hard to climb a mountain in the ocean? I think it might be very hard!

Mountains come in different types like:

-Volcanic

-Fold

-Fault-block

-Dome

-Plateau

Do you know what these words mean? Not to worry! We will talk about them in Chapter 1 of this book.

Remember: Mountains are very special places and we can learn lots of amazing things about them. They are also beautiful to watch and fun to explore. Please join me to on this quest to discover more on the wonderful world of ... **Beautiful Mountains!**

Chapter 1: Types of Mountains

Mountains are beautiful but they can be dangerous too. First let's talk about how important mountains are and then we will learn why we need to be careful if we want to explore them.

Mountains offer protection to many animals. It is a safe place for animals to hide and take care of their little babies. Some animals that live on the mountains are:

-Goats

-Gorillas

-Sheep

-Brown bears

-Antelope

-Lions

-Coyote

-Eagle

-Deer

-Leopards and many more!

Did you know mountains help to make rain and snow? Want to know how? This is how it works: When air travels around the Earth's mountains, the air gets stopped and sent into the sky, above the mountain. When the air gets high enough it becomes clouds and clouds turn it into rain and snow. Pretty neat… don't you think?

Lots of good water comes down from the mountains and feeds the rivers. But mountains are smart. When they collect water they don't let it go at the same time…. that would be a disaster!

So how do mountains hold the water until they can let it go in a safe way? Simple! It turns the water into snow and ice. And when it gets warmer, the mountains release the snow and ice a little bit at a time.

All of the most important rivers in the world flow from the mountains. Rivers like the Rio Grande and the Nile River get their water from mountains.

Rivers are not the only one who needs the mountains for fresh water. Guess who else needs them? Did you guess people? You are right!

We all need fresh water to live and mountains are a great place to get clean water.

Let's talk about the different kinds of mountains and how each one is special.

Volcanic mountains: You probably know that volcanic mountains are formed by volcanoes. This happens when hot rocks called magma push up through the earth's crust. When it cools, it looks like a cone made of rock. When more hot rocks push up, it forms a layer over the cone made of rock. After a while… layers on top of layers pile up until a volcanic mountain is born! Mount Pinatubo in the Philippines is a volcanic mountain.

Fold mountains: Fold mountains are easy to find. Do you know why? Because fold mountains are the most common type of mountain on planet earth. These mountains are born when two Tectonic plates collide and get all crumpled up. The neat thing about fold mountains is how they stretch out for miles and miles. The folds that climb up the mountain are called **anticlines**. And the folds that climb down the mountain are called **synclines**. The Swiss Alps and the Himalayas are Fold Mountains.

Fault-block mountains: These come from cracks, called fault lines, in the earth's crust. Some of the rocks and dust fall into the earth but some of it stays on top. Then big cracks appear and the rocks start to pile up on each other. An example is the Sierra's, a mountain range found in Nevada, and the Harz Mountains which are found in Germany.

Dome mountains: A dome mountain happens when hot rock under the surface starts to push up but it doesn't spill out on top. It stays in the ground. The area that pushes up is called a dome because it looks like half of a ball. The Black Hills in South Dakota are dome mountains.

Plateau mountains: These mountains take a long time to form and they are flat and look like tall squares or buildings. Over time, rivers and streams run through the plateau and form many interesting designs. The Tibet plateaus and the Altiplanos of South America are plateau mountains.

Test your skills!

Mountains have lots of interesting parts. This list is adapted from the Ducksters.com website. Let's see how many of these names you know…are you ready?

Crag: This is a group of rocks that sticks out from a cliff or rock.

Horn: This is a pointed peak formed by lots of glaciers.

Glacier: They are formed as snow continually freezes into ice, and keeps stacking up.

Face: This part of the mountain is steep and hard to climb.

Peak: This is the highest part of the mountain.

Ridge: This is a narrow path on the top of the mountain or the tops of many mountains.

Slope: These are the sides of the mountain.

Cirque: This shape looks like a bowl. It is formed by the head of a glacier and is usually at the base of the mountain.

Arete: When two glaciers melt on the sides of a mountain it forms a ridge that is narrow. This is an Arete.

Pass: This is between two mountains and it can be a valley or just a road to travel cross.

Did you recognize any or all of the names?

Good job!

Mountains have many different types of biomes. Do you know what a biome is? **Kids Discover Online** explains it in a simple way:

"Scientists divide the world into large natural areas called biomes. Desert and rainforest biomes are two that you've probably heard of. Each biome is known for certain kinds of plants and animals. But what's really at the heart of a biome is its climate. How hot or cold is it? How much rain and snow fall every year?"

What kind of biomes can we find on mountains? You might find a temperate forest, tundra, grassland, or taiga. But what makes each biome special?

Find out in chapter 2!

Chapter 2: Mountain Climates

Mountains have interesting climates where temperature and moisture are important to keep everyone alive!

The temperature can be hot, hot, hot and then cold, cold, cold. And the higher up you climb, the colder it gets. The weather can also change very fast. There might be a clear, beautiful sky and all of a sudden… booming thunder starts to echo and a storm soaks you with rain. This can happen in just one hour!

The reason has a lot to do with the biomes and the type of forests on the mountains. At the end of chapter 1 we talked about biomes and what they mean. Now let's learn about the different types and how they change the weather on the mountains.

Temperate forest: Did you know this forest gets its name from the temperature? Yes! That's what temperate means. It has nice temperatures and doesn't get too cold or too hot. There is lots and lots of rain in this type of forest but the soil is great for growing plants.

These forests also have four seasons: spring, summer, fall, and winter. Mountain lions, bears, fox, squirrels, timber wolves, and birds all live in temperate forests.

Temperate forests have beautiful trees like cypress, juniper, pine, cedar, fir, and redwoods. They also have broad or large leave trees like maple, chestnut, hickory, walnut, oak, and elm trees.

Plants grow in layers and lose their leaves during winter.

Temperate forests are found in the mountains of: Japan, China, North America, Australia, Europe, and New Zealand.

Tundra: this type of forest is very different. It is cold, cold, cold with no trees and the temperature can drop to -18°F. Brrrrrrrrrrr!!!!

This does not mean that it doesn't get warm during summer but the summer days do not last long. Lots of snowfall in the tundra and below the soil there is something called permafrost. Have you heard of this name before? It simply means that the ground under the top layer of soil is frozen solid… all year long!

You can probably guess that not many things grow in the Tundra so the land doesn't have a lot of trees and animals. Can you guess why? Yes…it is hard to live there and survive.

There are some things that grow in the tundra. Grass, shrubs, and herbs grow but they do not grow very big. Some animals live in the tundra like the artic hare, the artic fox, the snowy owl, and the musk oxen.

Did you know that some of the animals that live on the tundra change the color of their coat to white?

Tundra forests are found in the mountains of: Greenland, Canada, Scandinavia, Siberia, Russia, and the United States.

Grasslands: these types of forests can be a mixture of temperate and tropical, which are called savannas. Lots of wildflowers and grass grow in these forests. The summer can be hot and the winter can get cold.

Different types of animals live in the grasslands like: wolves, turkeys, fox, geese, bobcats, and smaller animals like snakes, mice, and rabbits. Many years ago large herds of bison used to live on the plains in North America but not many are left today.

The grass on the grasslands have interesting names, there is blue mamma grass, switchgrass, buffalo grass, and needle grass. These forests are found in North America, South America, and Asia.

Taiga: The taiga forest can be a cold and dry place. It gets so cold the temperatures can drop to -60°F. That is even colder than the tundra!

Beautiful evergreen trees grow in this type of forest. Do you remember what evergreen trees are? In our book **Beautiful Trees**, we explained:

"There are two main types of trees. Those that lose their leaves during the changing seasons and those that keep their leaves green all year long.

-The ones that lose their leaves are called: **Deciduous.**
-The ones that stay green all the time are called: **Evergreen.**

Evergreen trees do lose leaves from time to time but it always makes new leaves before the old ones fall off! This is how it can stay green all the time."

The taiga forest is full of evergreen trees but they don't have a lot of time to grow. Some trees have 12 months, other trees have 6 months but in the taiga forest, trees only have around 3 months to grow. This short time means trees work very hard to get as much growing done in the short time.

The evergreen trees in the taiga are fir, pine, cedar, and spruce. Under these beautiful trees are berries, ferns, and mosses. Squirrels, some birds, and insects live in the taiga but it is not an easy life.

These forests are found in the mountains of: North America and Scandinavia.

DID YOU KNOW?

The word "Taiga" comes from a Russian word that means: Forest.

Mountains are full of amazing things but there is still lots more we can learn about them! How would you like to become a mountain explorer? Here is a great way to get started.

Become a Mountain Explorer!

Quizzes can be a fun and exciting way to learn. This quiz is adapted from **Easy Science for Kids,** and can be done online. Don't forget to get permission from a guardian or your parents before searching or doing any activity online!

1- The _____ are on top of underwater volcanoes.

a-Hawaiian Islands

b-Rings of fire

c-Coral reefs

d-Rocky Mountains

2- What kind of buildup under the ground makes a mountain?

a-Sediment

b-Magma

c-River rock

d-Basalt

e-Lava

3- What kind of mountains are pushed to the surface by underground lava?

a-Dome mountains

b-Tectonic mountains

c-Fault block mountains

d-Volcanic mountains

4 - How long ago did the Himalayan Mountains start to form?

a-12 million years ago

b-29,035 years ago

c-127,000 years ago

d-55 million years ago

e-30 million years ago

5-A _____ forms when tectonic plates crash into each other, but DON'T crumple up on the surface.

a-Meadow

b-Plateau

c-Plain

d-Mesa

6-A type of Block Mountain is the _____ mountains.

a-Blockanese

b-Adirondack

c-Black Hills

d-Teton

e-Himalayas

7- When two tectonic plates _____ mountains are born!

a-Settle next to each other

b-Pull apart

c-Slam together

d-Slide along each other

8-A mountain is any land mass that rises 1,000 feet above _____.

a-The nearest human settlement

b-The nearest forested area

c-The surrounding area

d-Sea level

9-How long does a mountain take to form?

a-Thousands of years

b-Decades

c-Hundreds of years

d-Millions of years

10-Some mountains are formed when _____ blow over and over again.

a-Geysers

b-Magma pools

c-Volcanoes

d-Sulfur springs

Find the answers at the end…. of the book!

Chapter 3: Fun facts!

I hope you are enjoying this book on Beautiful Mountains! Here are a few more neat facts:

- This study of mountains is called Orology.

- Mountains are beautiful places but it can also be dangerous. If you get too high, the oxygen can be too low and you will not have enough air to breathe. This is called a "death zone" and it is approximately 23,000 to 26,000 feet high. If you wandered into this part of the mountain, you could only be there for a few minutes before you lost consciousness. To stay so high, you would need to have oxygen tanks or bottles to breathe. Can you think of a mountain where it is too high to breathe by yourself? Did you think of Mount Everest? Great job!

-*Mount Everest:* this mountain is called the highest mountain in the world. It is 29,035 feet high and found in the Himalayan Mountain range. To get a better idea of the size, think of the Empire State building. It would take 20 buildings stacked on top of each other to reach the top of Mount Everest. Isn't that amazing? But Mount Everest is not the tallest mountain. If you start from the bottom of the sea, Mauna Kea, which is found in Hawaii, would be the tallest. This mountain is 33,474 feet tall but the part you can see is only 13,796 feet above the ocean!

- Mount Everest has many names. The natives from Tibet call it "Chomolungma." This means "Goddess Mother of the Mountains." It is also called Sagarmatha, which means "Forehead in the Sky."

-In 2003 the UN general assembly decided that December 11th is a good day for International Mountain Day. This day was chosen to help people think about how good mountains are and how we can take care of them.

-Mountains are found in many parts of the world and most of our fresh water comes from them.

- There are lots of tall mountains under the water but it is not easy to see them because they are so deep!

- A mountain range is a group of mountains all together and they can be over 1,000 miles long.

- The highest mountain in the solar system is on planet Mars. It's a giant volcano called Olympus Mons.

-Many people live around mountains and love to look at them. How about you?

Vocabulary: Mountains are amazing objects in nature. Here is a small list of vocabulary words to help you learn more.

-Peak

-Moraine

-Leeward side

-Ridge

-Slope

-Geology

-Ledge

-Helmet

-Unexplored
Terrain

-Slither

-Acclimatization

-Canyon walk

-Biosphere

-Descent

-Dank

-Headwall

-Massif

-Highpoint

-Felsenmeer

-Gendarme

-Crevasse

-Cornice

Do you know what these words mean? If you are not sure, ask your parent or a guardian's permission to search for the definition online. I hope you learn something new!

(*www.dictionary.com*)

Conclusion:

In conclusion:

Our planet is full of wonderful things and mountains are an amazing part of the world around us. And even though we don't know everything there is to know about them, let's keep on learning. Imagine what amazing things we might discover someday.

Mountains are a big part of life and very important. They help with rains from the sky, they can stop storms from getting too strong, and they offer protection to animals and people. Mountains are also lots of fun to climb and explore!

There are tons of fun activities we can do on mountains. This can be mountain biking, walking, exploring, bird watching, hiking, and even river rafting. Which activity do you like best?

What else can you do?

Do you live near a mountain or a park with mountains? Why not ask your parents or your guardian to take you there? You can look up the location online and see what kind of mountain it is. Is it a plateau, volcanic, dome, or fold mountain? Then you could use a map and a notebook to explore.

If you do not like the idea of climbing or exploring mountains, why don't you learn more about the wildlife that live on them? It could be mountain goats, mountain lions, or another kind of animal.

One more idea!

If you decide to explore a mountain you might see strange trees or beautiful flowers you have never seen before. Why don't you take a picture and try to find out more about it? You could even use it for show and tell at school. Or you might decide to share it with friends and family. Whatever choice you make, have fun!

If you don't like the ideas in this book, put on your thinking cap and come up with your own conclusions. I am sure you will do an amazing job. We hope you have enjoyed this book on Beautiful Mountains. And remember…

"Educating the mind without educating the heart is no education at all." - Aristotle

Happy Learning!

Mountain Explorer Quiz Answers

1. Hawaiian Islands

2. Lava

3. Dome mountains

4. 55 million years

5. Plateau

6. Teton

7. Slam together

8. The surrounding area

9. Millions of years

10. Volcanoes

Sources:

http://www.primaryhomeworkhelp.co.uk/mountains/types.htm

http://easyscienceforkids.com/all-about-mountains/

https://online.kidsdiscover.com/unit/biomes

http://www.ducksters.com/science/ecosystems/temperate_forest_biome.php

http://easyscienceforkids.com/fun-mountains-quiz-free-general-knowledge-science-quiz-for-kids-online/

http://thegreenparent.co.uk/articles/read/5-facts-about-mountains/

http://science.nationalgeographic.com/science/earth/surface-of-the-earth/mountains-article/

Author Bio

K. Bennett loves to write for both children and adults. Many subjects are interesting to research, but writing for children is special to her heart.

Her favorite pastimes include reading, traveling and discovering new things. Each of these activities helps to fuel her imagination and acts like a blank canvas waiting for more stories.

She is intrigued with fantasy elements like hidden worlds and faraway lands. And basically anything that gets her imagination soaring to new heights!

Her writing credits include children books online, short stories for online magazines, and novellas listed at Amazon.com

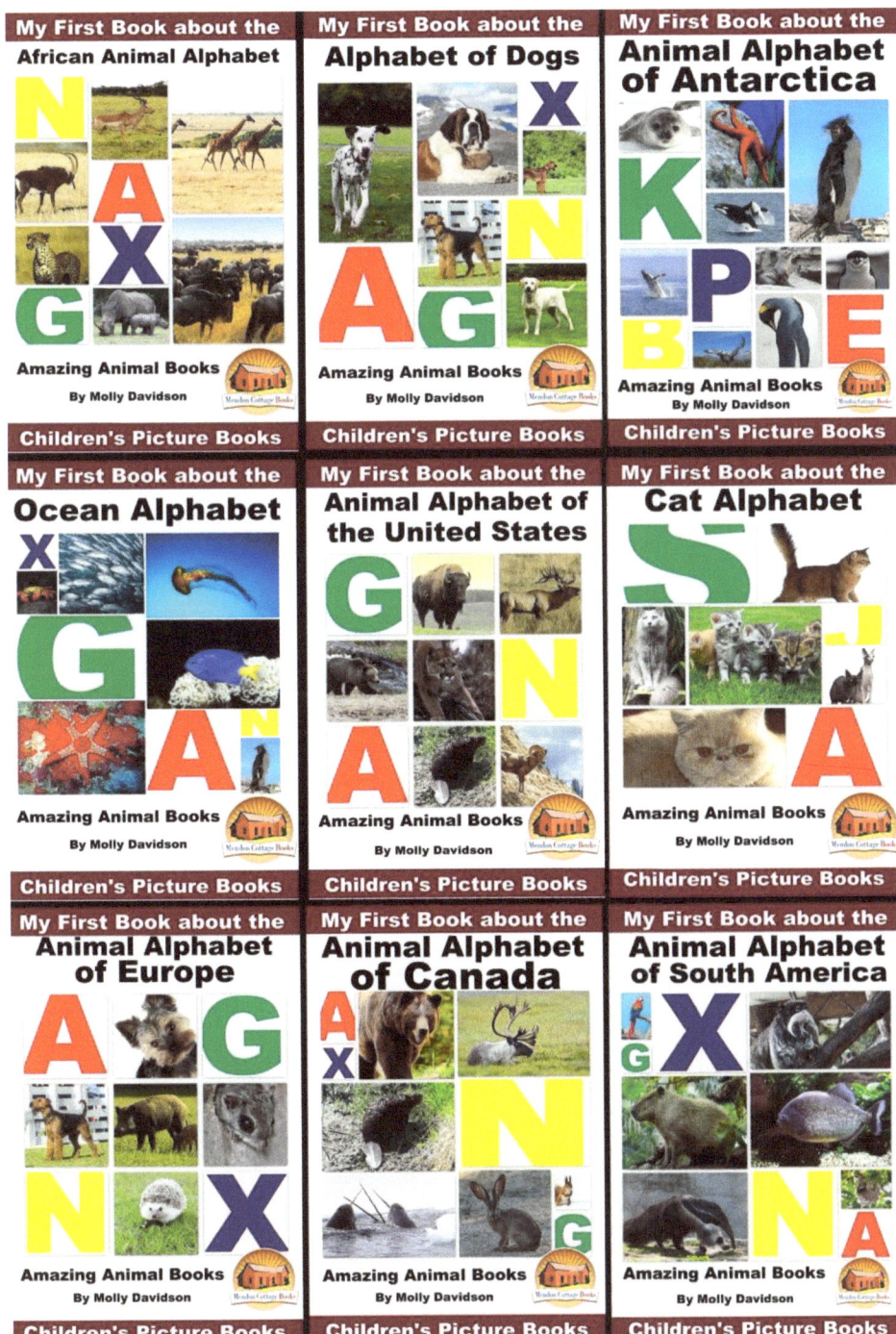

Our books are available at

1. Amazon.com

2. Barnes and Noble

3. Itunes

4. Kobo

5. Smashwords

6. Google Play Books

Download Free Books!
http://MendonCottageBooks.com

Publisher

JD-Biz Corp

P O Box 374

Mendon, Utah 84325

http://www.jd-biz.com/